W9-CLN-894

bush camp

bush camp

Marvin Francis

TURNSTONE ⬥ PRESS

Turnstone Press
Artspace Building
018-100 Arthur Street
Winnipeg, MB
R3B 1H3 Canada
www.TurnstonePress.com

Turnstone Press gratefully acknowledges the assistance of the Canada Council for
the Arts, the Manitoba Arts Council, the Government of Canada through the Book
Publishing Industry Development Program, and the Government of Manitoba through
the Department of Culture, Heritage, Tourism and Sport, Arts Branch, for our publishing
activities.

Cover image:: Marvin Francis
Cover design: Doowah Design
Interior design: Sharon Caseburg
Printed and bound in Canada by Friesens for Turnstone Press.

Library and Archives Canada Cataloguing in Publication

Francis, Marvin, 1955–

    Bush camp / Marvin Francis.

Poems.

ISBN 978-0-88801-324-8

    I. Title.

PS8561.R2586B88 2008   C811'.6   C2007-901885-8

For Samahra

Foreword

Marvin Francis is a difficult man to introduce. Poet, printmaker, spoken-word artist, scholar, archivist, humourist, provocateur—all of these labels describe him, but not fully, not adequately. As we can see in the opening pages of *bush camp*, Marvin enjoyed flouting labels through parody and irony and sometimes deadpan critique. He was a master at traversing boundaries, especially those of class and race and education. And because he moved so often between different worlds—from the Rez to the streets of Winnipeg to the halls of academe—he was able to produce a uniquely boundary-crossing art, one that situates his Cree culture very much in a contemporary, media-saturated, globalized, and commodified landscape. This ability marks him as one of the most innovative and compelling recent voices in Canadian literature.

Marvin's celebrated first book of poems, *city treaty*, charted new territory in its examination of Canada's urban Aboriginal voices and histories. Given that more than half of Canada's Native population now resides in cities, such a project was long overdue, and Marvin's approach to the subject is both experimental and highly memorable. Chock-full of wordplay, proliferating allusions and deliberate misinterpretations, *city treaty* is a scintillating, endlessly inventive book. At the same time, it articulates a powerful and often hilarious critique of the colonial ideologies that have led to the displacement of Native people in Canada's rural as well as urban spaces. The poems in *city treaty* become more complex with each reading, and as readers begin to follow the threads of allusion and juxtaposition, what emerges is a polyphonic document of contemporary Native culture in Canada.

Fans of *city treaty* and Marvin's other work—such as his live performances and his extraordinary visual art—were eagerly anticipating his follow-up poetry collection. There were rumours that he was working on a companion piece to *city treaty*, and the expectations for that new work were very high. I am happy to say that *bush camp* is that long-awaited new book, and that it is every bit as entertaining and complex as *city treaty*. But this is also a terribly sad occasion, because Marvin is not here to celebrate the book's publication. He died, far too young, in January of 2005, just after completing the manuscript of *bush camp*. His passing was a shock to all of his friends, colleagues, and fans, and it is still hard to believe that he is no longer with us. Marvin had so much more creativity to share with the world, so much more humility and sly humour that could have enriched our communities for a long time to come. But he also accomplished so many extraordinary things in his short time, and *bush camp* is an eloquent testament to that. It is a first-rate work of art in its own right, and it is also a wonderful reminder of the talent and commitment and the amazing generosity that Marvin embodied in his daily life.

bush camp is indeed a companion piece to *city treaty*, as the rumours indicated. It bridges gaps between urban and rural, Native and non-Native, Canada and the world. It also follows up on some of the most important themes of the first book, and I would like to examine one of those thematic parallels in some detail here. In *city treaty*, one of Marvin's abiding concerns is labour, especially the labour of Aboriginal people within the economy of colonial Canada. He writes about the (undervalued) work of Native trappers during the fur trade, and about the (unpaid) work performed by Native symbols and cultural artifacts that are used by corporations to sell consumer items. He also reveals how Native people are encouraged or even forced to sell their own identities in a contemporary multicultural marketplace. In all of these situations, the Native people are sold short, or sold out, by the economic and political bosses who manipulate the situation for their own advantage. *city treaty* reminds us that colonization was, and remains, even more an economic system of inequity than a political one.

In *bush camp*, Marvin's interest in labour is visible in the motley cast of working-class characters who labour on that most iconic of Canadian national symbols, the railroad. Johnny and Jenny and the Bull Cook and Frenchie might be seen as the latter-day heirs of John A. MacDonald's dream, which was to unify the country, to tie it together with bands of steel. But today that steel is rusting and bending; it is in dire need of maintenance. The railroad is no longer a place of grandiose dreams—it's just a place where a lot of hard and dirty work needs to be done.

bush camp can be read as a response to the high-blown rhetoric of E. J. Pratt's epic poem "Towards the Last Spike," which was once considered to be the canonical poem of Canadian nation-building. Pratt's poem focuses on the political leaders and the engineering team who planned the C.P.R., and it gives virtually no attention to the mostly non-white labourers who actually built it. In contrast, the protagonists of *bush camp* are not the elites, the epic hero-types. They are average Joes and Josephines who work because they need to pay off debts. One of them happens to be an Indian. They don't dwell upon the historic and symbolic implications of their work (they don't get paid to do that, and besides they don't have time). But nonetheless, Johnny must be aware at some level that he is working on the same railroad that in effect created Canada, that brought Canadian troops to the West in 1870 and 1885, and that brought hordes of settlers who displaced Native people from their lands. In *bush camp*, the railroad is The Man, a.k.a. The System, a.k.a. colonization. But despite the fact that Johnny and his fellow workers are cogs in that enormous wheel, they manage to forge something precious and beautiful from their work together. What they make is community. How they make it is through comradeship and mutual trust and sometimes even love.

bush camp is quintessentially a love story, a romance featuring the unlikely iconography of spikes and hammers and cowpokes and missiles. The love between Johnny and Jenny maintains a sense of beauty, an optimism in the poem, despite the macho setting and despite the fact that these workers are surrounded by threats of violence and inequity and environmental degradation. This is, after all, a poem of war as well as love. The "bush camp" where Johnny and Jenny work shares its name with the "camp" of George W. Bush and his allies, who have been all too willing to deploy cruise missiles (sometimes called Tomahawks) and other weapons in their attempts to colonize yet another region of the globe. By invoking this sly double-naming, Marvin Francis suggests that the railroad bush camp is not isolated from the rest of the world at all; it is in fact intimately connected. The military-industrial complex that targets Iraq is also found in the muskeg-soaked wilderness of western Canada. The imperialist aggression that displaced Native people from their land is still at large, both in Canada and abroad. But Johnny and Jenny's love defuses the threat, at least partially. When Jenny brings flowers to the cruise missile, it is a sign that things are going to be different in this bush camp.

So in one sense, this book is about how ordinary people can resist the machinations of power and ideology by trusting in the things that make us human: compassion, and humour, and affection. This is why *bush camp* is finally a story of hope, even though it was written in the shadow of war and during the author's final illness. I like to think of it as a distillation of Marvin Francis's fundamental generosity of spirit, which was immediately visible to anyone who knew him.

There are so many other paths to follow in *bush camp*, so many marvels to discover. I leave that pleasure to you. For anyone seeking advice on how to approach the book, I would say: follow the hints, the half-suggestions. Read with your hunches on full alert. Backtrack early and often. Like in the bush, or in the cement wilderness of the city, there is always more to find here.

Warren Cariou

bush camp

(a warmup poem)

the unparalleled imagination of a bush camp
nickname

see that guy over there, leaning against the sheet
metal, that guy, you know, the skinny-tall one,
that one usually alone always chewing on something

his **s** nickname is

t

r

e

t

c

h

and that high rigger before, during, and after
work, our Casanova, sez he is from Quebec, we call
him

Frenchie

and way down over there, the hotshot, crazy-assed
welder from St. John's, his name is

Newfie

the ornery, forklift operator with the red hair?
that is

Red

And, of course, any Native guy on site, usually the
laborer, it just may be the 1970s in this poem
after all, he can be playing hockey, cruising the
bar, slow walking down the street, or just
workin', his nickname, guaranFUCKINGteed, has gotta
be

←↑↓
chief

if you do anything that resembles
reading/righting/dreams you just may be called

perfessor

so then, if you were
sayyyyyyyyyyyyy
a red-haired, skinny-tall dude, doing some writing,
and were the last of the Beothuks

you would be
stretch-red-perfessor-newfie-chief

much too complicated   guys would beat you up for
that

keep it simple stupid
or you end up as the one holding the dumb end of
the measuring tape
or if you don't come from the same home town
always from outta town, different reference point
then   not a popular mechanic
U get to clean up that diesel spill   no rags
in sight and you find a way (quietly use the
mechanic's spare coveralls) your boots get no place
to dry   maybe your gloves nailed to a wall
Or, traditionally to a tie this spiked leather
unfashionable
or maybe some biggish, older guy would send you to
the foreman   with obvious sideways glance

for sky hooks
or that construction classic
the board stretcher   guys get too bored they might
pick on you   ask you goofy questions   probe
for something to do
and that might become your name
few formal introductions on the   gang

but
after a long, long time on the gang, say about a
month, everyone will gradually fit their notches
you know where to eat   did some laundry   used
to sounds at night   knew the pecking order

(He stood way back in his white hard hat, kodiak
leather confident on the outside   wondering
                          who this woman is
                            all the way inside
              trying to think of a nickname for her
                                        otherwise
                    the bush camp balance would
                        mean less work done

he decides that a woman in a bush camp
any woman   no matter what   is called
        Goddess)

                I think.

                I know.

welcome to

bush camp: a longer poem

everyone was afraid to wake her so off they went
to work without her, railroad metal noise somehow
tamer, and she sleeps through the uneasy glances at
her door no problem   cuz jenny was from the south
and this was the north
and her southern dreams
fit the pillow of north

and she lets the past   dream her present

she has the gig cuz she is there wearing a northern
t-shirt in a northern way cuz Johnny taught her how
to muskeg
in a big way, of course

The Muskeg Series

Johnny Muskeg

Johnny Muskeg never
met Mustang Sally
or especially Muktuk Annie
nor dare he think of Peggy Sue
but nevertheless Johnny
began to look for a wife

Cash Cow (a business poem)

It was too easy to rip
off Johnny's cash
first time in town
all screwed up on an escalator

Advice for Northerners

when you go to town
don't brag, don't mention
how good you are with an axe
trust me on this one
time to trade in the gum
boots even new ones

Advice for Johnny Muskeg

> when looking for a wife
> Gum Boots = No Wife
> John approaches women on escalator
> they are surprised at his difference
> but gum boots tip the scale
> (rubber and mud)
> John sleeps alone that night

Going to the Boot Store

Can I help you!
the sort of boots women like
so I can get married

You need these boots for riding? or for show?
I ride without saddle ride for the wind I ride
freehorse

These are perfect if you have the cash
I need leather I must walk thru silent stare

Fits like downtown not the burbs
better learn new dance
new drums new boots!

Jenny

Jenny also goes to town looking
something new in men
but was from the south
vague in mind not spirit in her
quest has money has time
reads captivity narratives with red eyes
hates escalators and especially gum
boots on a man
but
Jenny
needs dancing shoes

        Johnny finds some grub

Do you have a reservation?
        Yeah, it's up north

What is your preference?
        Sit me by that table full of girls
        let me buy them lunch the northern
            way
It is a smoky section
        Bring friendly tea for all. Muskeg tea.
I am sure we can substitute, sir.

(slurp, stare, slurp, stare)

Thanks for the tea, mister, weird as you are

Allow me north talk not visitor slang
but muskeg soft

> What kind of tea *isss* this?
> *D-9 Cat sinks, muskeg wins*

We're all married at this table, mister!

> *I need your words to be pliable to*
> *make me fit for love*

your   new boots dance
            surprisingly

Jenny Destroys her Old clothes

right there downtown threw her
old clothes away her universe
the duffel bag
next, dancing shoes
no glass slipper   no way to tell
and Jenny
feels good like spring feels
walks portage ave flow
not too fast not lost not scared
not in any hurry   that is Jenny walking
down the street
enough money to walk her way
value immense clothes she picks all by herself
      pushes

            Jenny down   the town

11

Frog Corner at Rush Hour

John and intersections have clashes
frankenmetal rushes film
hop across then hop back
and breathe deep and look for wife
gasoline romance cement love electrical sex neon
no wife John asleep   alone   that night

The Last Resort

every town has one
open late drink darkly
no names not once no one cares no nothing
Jenny checks it out then
splits
because Jenny keeps cool

Alley Poem

this one alley
just off albert street
has this **L** shape
graffiti smell the
short cut to the donut joint
walk this alley watch
the corners walk big
Johnny enters alley from one side

Jenny approaches other end
sniffs
keeps walking

Johnny must try harder.

diesel generator poem

rumblllllllllllerrrredneeeeckskin I can't hear a
freaking damn thing   what did he say
1/2 trillion moosepower later
diesel poetry for deaf ears
oil patch critics wrench words
that diesel cough over water over railroad space
carries far
Jenny wakes up thinking of the john
envelops the reality of metal walls   a single
bunk   a desk   a lamp a couple of sticky-almost
skin zines   a sardine can ashtray

some empty coke cans lonesome in the   corner   the
spring sun   a hairy grey blanket with a red stripe
a pillow with unidentified stuffing   the
secret agent of pillows apparently   a locker
that had been drunk smashed   a sawn steel rail
lurks like an anvil   then she finds a readers
digest   way outdated   she reads leisurely 'I am
Joe's lung'
and feels completely at home
and then the hesitant   disquieting   mouse

shydoor sounds

and since she slept in exhausted jeans
Jenny
quick opens the door

standing there   part of the bunkhouse landscape
mops for friends   hot water control the loudest
weapon in his arsenal
a man who loves the gang
standing short
squinting in the shade of the bunk cars
anxiety wrinkles permanent
there stands the
artery of the bush camp   the bull cook

bull cook poem

too old to swing a hammer
too young to die
working scars made soft by detergent vibes
the bull cook behind the scenes mopping fool
anonymous bottom of the line
tells small railroad town drunk stories   told
only at night in draft beer episodes
has great connections with the cook   with the
white hats   with the dispatcher   with all of the
hat colors
(Jenny thinks of how Johnny once painted his hard
hat red and how, for awhile at least,   everyone

14

thinks he is some kinda specialized diesel mechanic
or something, cornered some respect almost)

has tools hidden strategically   keys for every
freaking thing

can turn off the hot water   can turn on the
industrial disease   avoids the real heavy lifting
but the bull cook knows there is **no** such thing as

I can't

I can't lift that
I can't work overtime
I can't stand the smell of his sox
I can't eat this shit no more
I can't believe they put saltpetre in the food
I can't live in a world without women
I can't feel my frozen digits
I can't make it to my days off

He knows.

Jenny has craggy tea with him and learns all this
by noon.

She knows she is not working in the kitchen with
that crazy fuck cookwannabe who slaps greasy eggs
like a fifties greaser (without the muscle car)
onto the plate in front of her and goes back to his

freezer where strings of wieners trod under twist
like mystery meat snakes (like his scraggly
moustache)

She takes her paperwork and changes the job
description from cook's helper (called the cookie
on most gangs) to machine operator first class
[writers division pencilled in the 'other'
section], whatever the hell that is and goes back
to her bunk with some smuggled corn flakes and
coffee and picks up a moose-eared western beckoning
from a shelf alongside outdated newspapers (moose-
eared = a northern, ask van herk, she knows) and
settles in until the gang returns, happy
Alone, until that passenger train hurtles silver
not too far from her bunk at eighty clicks, from
her head where she dreams, and she wonders why
there is no slow order, and thinks about the
competing silver of the propane cars and the casual
way the train crews experience death at a crossing

waiting for the passenger

bandanna sweat mood   watch some of the guys
            hang rats for the passengers

       some secret hope for a little glimpse of something
         something female or clean or a little happy
                besides the railroad
                where gravel is ballast

and where Agent Orange right of way attacks
anything green
creosote black   working on the gang
John Henry got all the press

Johnny Muskeg had no time to remember
he didn't
"get in   get rich   get out"

he was already there
he was poor
and
he loves the muskeg

where contractor dreams watch the D-9
sink funding money
sink industrial   a natural submarine of soft

Johnny went south
trapper intensity
in the bush of the

city
camp

road tripping

the oldest road trails
johnnycakejohnnytakejohnnycake the latest young
traveller
that mind opening
you are really on your own
baby
road trip from a south carolina park
to a chicago peanut bar

with this guy from the robert taylor homes
south side slum bigger than winnipeg

heavy vibes grabs his muskeg ass
can only be an experience
kentucky hiway 75 mph
moon shines like moonshine
not one driver's license in the car
they were all secretly hitchhikers
enough cash to party

cruise all the way to those thirsty peanuts
wrigley field hovers in background
sip americano beer
smoke chicago dope
watch those black kids swipe hub caps
fatal intersection
U better chuck some coin
how this is normal in this hood

urban stories sit up all nite
baseball bat keeps rats off the baby
no bush to hide in
nowhere to run
tough stupid rules

slide thru the chicago bus depot
a day or two after the bomb went off
nobody notices, cares, or wants to see
that big hole in the floor
johnny's chicago scene empties
desire to be big city cool
he hits the alberta trail
tells jenny this story

when they
sitaloneatnitemeettwentyfourjointtalkcoffeesmokelov
eeeeeeeeeeeee

together

fire extinguisher fight

it all starts when Red gets sick and goddam tired of listening to

Frenchie brag, brag about his real, bush-mirage, and been too long

in the bush hallucinatory women and how they always pick him

out, bragging about having sex in his transam (a cock and trull

story) in the train station parking lot: *she couldn't wait* sez Frenchie

cracking another beer, looking around for approval

(he's not driving nothing this year thinks Red, transam my ass!)

Frenchie bragging how the women   always single him out

from all those other drinking yahoos in that crowded never been

this busy for a long long-time prairie bar

from the local yokel who had a hot car but no money

from her passed – out – for the count boyfriend (cuz most

small town girls got one boyfriend or two or more counting all the

handy nearby small towns)

from the reality of TV

from the other denizens of the bar, the farmer who had no one but

his land, the small town hardware store owner, a shriner wannabe

who imagines his nail and tool empire entitles him to all the

accessible women, the last mink rancher in the area who hires kids

to do all the grisly work, and forgets to pay them and goes to this

bar instead, the unemployed guy who has a shrinking group of allies, the section guys in their own section talking shop, the guy

hauling gravel with no contract,   the proudfear of first timers

And in another saloon cosmos, sorta of the red planet of beer sec-

tions, from that dark corner section   the browning version

of honky-tonk

The Native Table .   taboo cooler   can't sit there and be

all white

where beer and money were the only exchange district

in between was a definite border

           far from invisible   barb wire neighbor

                        bi-culture vulture perimeter

the jukebox was the demilitarized zone

white contra red

the music sporadic from Merle Haggard to Smiling Johnny and the

Wildcats (U mean U never heard of this famous half-cut, weird/

polka-inspired music? you must be from TO, or LA, or worse)

only their money was welcome   beer slammed down on table

dying to cut you off service with

no smile

           no other bar in town

                        off sales sure sounds better

After the bar slams down, closed   last call : no mercy

then blind you with lights, took all your money

they all were drinking in the washcar

24s sprawled liked drunks on top of the sinks open packs of

smokes beckon rather than hidden under hard hat none for you

monday morning presence

smoky bush camp currency   legal tough not tender.

Jenny keeps bush quiet in this male driven world of elusive mating.

She sat on the washer while the guys automatically bowed to her

every whim. The gurgle jug of laundry under her ass wasn't bad so

she stays to hear their after bar stories. She misses Johnny.

Now that Frenchie, hits on every woman he meets and gets the

guys in trouble.

Earlier that night Red gets a few shots in the face, has to eat some

crow, cuz of that prairie casanova

But even a railroad gang has to back up against the wall together

Left alone you get   **sniped**

Red knew he shoulda let them shit-kick Frenchie : *he was just*

drunk, not good enough, does not count in the hotel parking lot, late nite

after bar closing → the killing hour

Red sips slowly, not as drunk U think, waits, the party is not over yet.

Jenny never usually wanders to the bar with them   *how aboutta kiss?*

Toro likely when the booze monster catches the drunk train   the

lonely guy gets rock hard plain

She could drink for free all nite long just by being at the table

They pound spikes for this? thinks Jenny, as she can tell some of
them will be broke at layoff time   work all spring all summer
all fall into the first snow
And
sleeping in the sally ann by December
working that industrial overload
I froze my fingers for minimum wage endings.
Jenny tries not to be too aware of those insistent voices, hidden
voices, just at the edge of the railroad trax, most of the gang doesn't
stray too far from the track, aware of the bears, those bears were
kinda wild, not like benevolent banff bears, these bush bears spook
real easy. These voices from the bush, loud and proud murmur-
probe all the day and most of the night dreams.
She senses the watching eyes, the circling minds, beyond her realm,
feels them looking into and through her   while the drinking,
lonely guys are not in tune   except degrees of hangover
but Jenny feels no fear.
Sober, all of the guys on the gang are gentlemen extraordinaire,
glad for a word, something friendly, just for anything that isn't
soaked in creosote, or whiskers.
They are kinda like the cowboys of the Old West
she thinks about Johnny's stories
of hammer handle fights
of gang 101 pulling into town   after a long haul   with two
dead

you were on your own when the red fleet gang moves   days alone

up north travel time   no white hats

survivor measures   ambushes in minaki

disguised as a rock cut   seismic camouflage

But the gang, all of them drifters in their own way, small town

guys, Natives, Portuguese fresh from Angola, drunks, wanderers,

adventurers, transients, college hopefuls, fugitives, mostly male,

mostly blue collar, hail from somewhere else, nomad runaways,

mainly broke when you work on the gang except for the lifers,

those who got old, got sober

some had no where to go and were happy to eat, do laundry for

free, pay no rent   some had wall-thumping nightmares

others just kept to work/eat/sleepeeat/workkkk/sleep/eat and

eeeeeeat some more

cuz meal times were sorta social   many put on weight

got weird   ate off alone in the corner   glaring outward

time for a day off

working overtime moving those infamous   painted red

outhouses (some were two holers)   new genre: biffy comedy

that train comes hurtle-hurry down the track like always

these new guys, guided by an eighteen year old assistant foreman,

cuz his old man was a freaking supervisor, therefore hated

drop the red shithouse that they were moving right onto the track

and run panic-assed, the irresistible passenger train hits it dead-on,

nobody gets hurt

but U **never delay** the passenger

the passengers press faces against the disbelief of this outrage

in doubt one tourist throws them money like they do off the
cruise ships

the foreman's first clue that something was wrong

that particular rattle that pieces of shithouse make when they
bounce off his bunk

followed quickly by a disgruntled train conductor on the radio

and the hapless assistant foreman's meek appearance

but Hey! It was overtime!

these shithouses had to be sturdy   more than once a bear kept

a guy trapped for hours at note, whiling away the shithouse blues

while a bear snuffles about at a leisurely pace, nosing for food,

happy to hang out

And as you get used to the smell (first sign of getting bushed: see

bushed poem later in this manuscript) and the bear, at night, might

or might not be seen, and any noise is bear-like and seems to be
too freaking close

wild schemes of escape enter this domain

like setting a whole bunch of toilet paper on fire, then … well,

uh…. or making fierce noises hoping nobody from the gang hears

(while secretly hoping that somebody does) accompanied by the

shrill, mock heroic

Fuck off you damn bear!

never works   doesn't translate into grizzly dialect

it was this group of guys who

                        place

                        her

                        gingerly

                        on

                        that

                        only

                        woman

                        in town

                        pedestal

–

INTERLUDE (poems that work overtime and get in the way):

going to see that tooth woman

going to see that tooth woman today
I owe her one hundred dollars
I want my tooth back instead

going to cash my tax money
I got it coming   you see
many ways to spend   one pocket

going to cash those beer bottles
original recyclers in frantic action
brown glass jobs pay good

gotta pay that tooth woman
pipeline silver
bush camp canary

ONE TOOTH WOMAN IN TOWN

(johnny scribbles this on cig pak while jenny peeks, sips 24 hour
joint coffee and realises she is happy in this memory)

But then Red   jumps up

gets up quick   beeline to a startled Fenchie and Red sudden

swings fist windmill

sneak attack punches hurt more

a right another right, two rights make a left, an uppercut

a right hook   mostly half cut   out of the blue

feeling blue   hurting blue

Frenchie who should be used to this

attitude adjusts tonite

brown bottles flash slow motion

the vets jump up and grab their beer   one smooth motion   back

off   back against the wash car wall

the inevitable foam and glass tornado gravity storm

most could see this coming   things were as they should be

the combatants have the necessary, starting words:

fuk U!

fuk U too!

Oh yeah? Fuk U and the horse U rode in on!

Yeah? Well, uhmm, go fuk a snake!

Biff! Bam! Bam Biff! Ouch fuk!   **etc.**

they started boxing real freaking

serious

and feeling macho-bored wanting to add their two bits worth

some of the onlookers, full of booze/boredom/hate their freaking

jobs

these others take sides, a bad sign at a party with mostly all guys

Except the transplanted native section, most of these guys on this

gang were from a rez close to the Thompson hiway, they had jobs,

they came back every spring, kept separately in a group and their

leader, a vet on the gang, decides who does what, worked best if

left to themselves   bunked together

walked to town in a bunch

                    they never, ever bitched about the food

Though once a disgruntled group of Native gang workers, treated

dirt, stopped the trains from running, the main line smoulders at a

sullen standstill, trains delayed in three provinces

                    an early roadblock

the white hats responsible were quietly shipped out to other gangs,

and the food got much better, and they had water in the wash cars

always now   now they merely watch, sipping slow,

survivor alert, a quiet chuckle, a drag on a hand rolled minimum

wage smoke   Jenny wishes she was sitting there

with them   they weren't posing,

            they were keeping cool

and then always in the centre of things

Stretch grabs somebody, throws him onto the floor, then he grabs a

handy fire extinguisher

        then lets that town guy know whose turf this is

             Who is this guy? Who does he think he is?

   the same guy that follows them back to the bunks after closing

         time uninvited, with no beer or smokes or nothing

Stretch, so quiet when sober, so rowdy when drunk

gives him an extra gang jolt   that red cylinder

always charged   puts out the fire of a punch

creamy white soda rage discharges

            fire extinguisher opera

and then coughing, let's get the fuck outta here, Jenny somehow

thru the door, runs to her own bunk, hides behind the tie crane,

when the clamorous charge of white hats whizzes by, with

disgruntled RCMP and the local dogs start to bark, something for

the whole town to talk about tomorrow morning, grist for that

extra gang hatred mill

         the same full mounties

who circled the bunks several times when we first got to town

got the message you extra gang bums?

they always checked the lists of men

looking stern

sometimes they dragged someone away

there was this one guy

to Jenny's amazement   gets himself arrested right on the track

accompanied by the jeers and cheap humour of the short run for

freedom (about three tracks worth, cuz the clumsy kid trips over a

claw bar)

and they cuff him   rub his face on the rail   a little bit

warn us to stay away from the bar tonite

while the suddenly impotent, powerless white hats give

conflicting orders

everyone takes an unscheduled smoke break to watch the show

a young kid wanted for armed robbery it turns out

this kid, attached to a burly cop, leads him right by that place

where dirty water discharges from the kitchen, that day we fixed a

switch close to the bunks

and this kid leads the cop   headed for the cop car perched

halfway in the ditch

the cop gets it dishwater glorious

drags the kid by the hair four hundred longest yards to the waiting

cop car

the kid got it back later in the cells

they paid for the damage, Frenchie and Red, sheepish, tease-assed
all day long by the old-timers   who were pissed off by the mess
and these old-timers laid the law down to the foreman, who
young and on the rise, who said nothing, he knew these old guys
had weight
the Road Master would take some of them aside and ask questions
he worked them hard that next day   but not too hard   just
what was expected
but they had something new to talk about today   everyone had a
different opinion of what happened
Frenchie took off that morning   left this note nailed on his wall

can I quit? The guys are all mad at me.
These are not good conditions.
I better go home, huh?
Frenchie
ps: tell them I will pick up my check in winnipeg

all was well once more as the beer sweats out, as the days off come
closer, as their tired bodies catch a third wind, and they think of
supper and sleep, at least this day was different
another closer to layoff time passes by in indifferent time
Jenny dreams another Johnny Gang Story

the old man and the pee

there is always a railway legend that happens in the startUp

spring usually where this loner/loser/drifter/semi-homeless/city

fucked opium, almost always, white guy, takes it into his tumble-

down-head to Israel close to where the gang is working, right close

to the railroad track where guys had to nip the black ties,   tamp

the black ties, carry those black ties, disturb the gunnysacks of an-

chors, root for spikes, muscle the angle bars, hug rusty in piles, hate

thrown from a gondola car, half buried, scrapes of crushed rock,

sometimes a keg of spikes rolls

iron-bounces into the cold spring driven water

sometimes deer skulls watch this activity

so, still, this freaking guy couldn't bother to piss further into the

bush even after some words spoken at coffee break (usually no cof-

fee breaks on the gang, but this is a poem) words that made every-

one else quiet, so this old man, the best spiker of the crew, worked

the gang all his life, a guy who almost got married in steel toed

boots and thought fuckall of it, this old man grabs his favorite spike

hammer, and a few black fly-bitten-disgruntled-brutal-labouring-

all-day-in-the-hot-sun   guys grab him,

lay him flat faceup, spread-sparrowed right in the middle of the

track, and this old man drove those steel spikes into his jacket, his

creosote designer jeans, spiked through his clothes into the gravel

frozen ties, one spike by his balls for railroad punctuation, full railroad hammer swings, three hits per spike

               the way you are supposed to

this city guy simmers, an urban fried egg, piss all dried up, cry

wishing, the bush can be street tuff too, his railroad crucifixion

bled extra gang reality, no colors on this gang, especially piss yellow,

except the hard hat hierarchy, that construction totem pole, yellow

always looks up, then a white hat came walk-in, hesitant close, starts

fishing kegs of spikes from the culvert creek, a few guys go to help

him, cuz that jobgig came stalkin

    walking down the track   two ties at a time

          the way you are supposed to

bushed

you can sense the guy who has been working too long

too hard

too much diesel, not enough wine

this is the guy who grows bristles almost visible, shaves the same

six whiskers every morning   when U get bushed U start to

eat alone   overeat, bitch about the food, and keep shovelling it

down   pushy in line   greedy

you just dare that white hat to say something, anything, ready to be

fired at any instant

you fantasize ways to get to town *I know, I'll step on a nail… maybe,*

no, no, I'll tell them I have crabs, they will have to get rid of me then, I'll catch some bugs tomorrow, that's it…and fake it

or I'll punch that cook's lights out!…. they might make me walk tho….

just freaking put me on top of that list of layoffs, cuz layoff means pogey,

quit means food bank… I can't take it no more no more

Jenny sees this guy, one that was a walking toolbox of small obscure

tools, the electrician brought in special, takes orders from nobody,

has an actual trade, has homemade customized coveralls: mostly

leather patches, has weird little pliers that do insoluble wire things

Just had

to have the nickname *Sparks*

🟥🟥🟥🟥🟥🟥

He had been on the site, always trouble with the complex signals

here, early in the spring, still snow, he was here before the cooks,

just he and the bull cook then watch as others arrive, one by one,

jump off the passenger, bewildered and broke, as many come and

go, everyday somebody quits or hires on

conveyer drifter belt taken in a few notches

Jenny was a vet after about two weeks, guys would quit and there

would be a race to see what they left behind

books, clothing, skin zines, a half bottle of whiskey, leather boot

laces scavenged, big value in bush camp.

Sparks started the season by politely asking people to pass him

things, condiments, tools

Now

Where's the mustard, fuck?

(same thing happens to everyone, this is the extra-gang

lord of the flies)

Now

he throws laundry like it is confetti, not sure what has been washed,

sleeps too often in oily coveralls, too much overtime

he was bushed

he secretly plotted to murder the bull cook

but took a day off instead

Meanwhile, Johnny learns the city ways.

New Crossing

Last nite on that late nite crowded sidewalk I saw this kid get

jacked for his stainless steel colored walkman, he should have Ran

Man, cuz cool hood guys are too cool, too smoked out, too aware

of the heat, to chase you for long, right up against the windows of

the portage place bus shack, I call this the madhattan bus transfer,

knew I should have got off at a different stop, there were about six

of them, all hood young, all part of this downtown mall culture,

the great economic hope of the last millennium, I know, let's build

a mall and put a fountain in it, a mall of portages from street to

jail to mall to street to long walk home in the hood late at nite,

this kid seemed to owe them money, he was scream silent looking young white boy, all alone, the many witnesses gather their wallets, their bags and some seem used to it, the buses landscape this new frontier like the canoes of old, they just keep paddling, barking gasoline disapproval, the smart ones catch the next bus no matter what, some keep walking, most have fear, let's build a mall and put a fountain in it, that will cure our downtown, the speed of this exchange is suddenly over, the street vibes slow down, the kid slipquiets away, the buses stop/go, mostly go, and I lean against a post, thinking about some mace-sidewalk-style, and pretty sure I would have seen it coming.

(much later in the poem)

push push in that bush

this year   this fall   I will tell

the geese not to fly south

but what do I tell my daughter

my precious daughter

the red the white the blue

pallet drips mostly red from long distance

my composition will hide and begin and end and shiver

the deepest corner of

the frame

this is the year that big time

money bucking movie export

tom crews   will be replaced

by cruise tom   a hawk

cnn green video shock

gotta keep up the new nazi oil stock

this is the last year where

marine   life   oxymoron over water

under the radar gun

push push that bush

err craft   air borne   air dying

that burning desert bush

jenny finds a cruise missile

sometime way back in time, like 70s (!?), they used to test the latest

in cruise missiles in muskeg country (come see the latest in

northern cruise ware) some older guys on the gang claimed they

saw them, same on the rez, but jenny was pretty sure that she

quietly had found one, now that they left her alone, and her job

was to count things, amount of material used   how much was

not used (there were farmers who built entire buildings out of
stolen ties, track jacks were hot items, a thirty-nine foot rail made a
helluvva beam for a house)
she just estimated and nobody knew the exact numbers here in the
bush (or anywhere else) and she knew that and so did the deeply
disturbed white hats

during that walk, that unusual bird sound, now thinks jenny, later,
maybe that was a mutant bird, a glide bird, and she remembers
unusual crow activity and she stopped getting lost in the bush
black plumage audio guide
everyone else only left the track for one, yellowish, purpose
alone out of eye shot

the light was perfect and there was enough metal behind the rust
to reflect and then jenny realises that this missile was not all rusted
70s style but pretty shiny like bait for a packrat

city tree

in town Johnny refuses to be lonely and approaches a woman on
yet another escalator
telling her: "I'm interesting"

I O, I O, it is off to work I go

Johnny investigates   stop-gap labor

finds the place   written on a piece of torn cig pack address

office entrance in an alley   hand painted sign: Extra Labor

outline line drawing of a hardhat, work boot thing, a hammer, no

tongs

there was a couple of young-haired guys playing checkers

        jiving/talking young tough/laughing

rolling smokes from that cheap, cut-your-own, natural tobacco

the wise staff shields themselves

bullet-proof glass   paper thrust furtively through a hole

they never go into the room where the guys hang out, gighoping,

bullshitting

      sometimes there was coffee

industrial jungle world

of Man Friday – Industrial Overload – Workin' Man

one-day gigs all labor all dirty   quick reflex work safety   the

usual dead end reality   killer heavy   shovel pesticides,

maybe in the 70s

weird industrial addresses that nobody could find, including the

freaked out cab driver   rust and dirt and smoke and oozing oil

heads   they gave U a two dollar bill for lunch and bus fare,

expenses, or fit five of you in a disgruntled cab

if U took off and pocketed that two dollar bill there was always this

one bespectacled guy who would always remember U, even five

years down the road

then the lowest I O for you, buddy toady, nothing nobody else

will hire you   gotta leave town for this one

it was at some foundry, that jinxed foreman, just a kid compared to

the I O guys, shaves his six whiskers every morning

for a while, he had them rolling empty forty-five gallon drums

back and forth aimlessly, loud and not so proud

the noise level hurting

the guys who had full time jobs at the foundry just shook their

heads and went about their business

this forekid didn't know what else to do   too scared and too

dumb to ask

he did a lot of pacing, instructing

by noon Johnny almost quit

the sacred and scared construction commandment: look busy!

make noise and dust and hide out in remote parts, usually

outdoors, in the weather the others hid out and avoided them

anyway and anyhow   rolling empty drums was easy

so we giggle   make eyes when the kid bellows orders
empty   metallic buck sixty an hour
noise and dust levels become patterns of interest   toxic payday
no dust masks, that bandanna always handy

then after another no-lunch where everyone avoids each other
corners quiet talk between drinking buddies
stories told to a kid just starting out   always punctuated by the
promise of up north
lotsa bullshit   going to fox creek   seismic line cutting   good money
need wheels to get there at two in the morning   snowing like hell and they
put us right to work fades away the need to cash his check hotel lobby
U need a thousand bucks to join that union and no job guaranteed, fuck!
that pool hall will cash a check   makes U buy a carton of smokes, weird
brands like sportsman, number 7, in vogue tobacco, this was when people
smoked players plain the strongest cigarette on the prairie (thus the world)
but he cashed that check   kind of like a chit, know what I mean?
so we drove all fucking night for nothing   we got there before the bunks
did, some more got off of the passenger and there was nothing there, man!
slept in the ditch with anchor sacks   then the A-holes dumped one of the
bunks unloading, showing up at five in the morning   diesel smell
stick grips the walls, man, like shit to cow pies,   the smell of mechanical
pre-death, you cannot get rid of diesel, it works its cancer-way into your
nose-bones and dribbles your brain on a hard court job

more guys than bunks   one guy goes home in a huff spinning

gravel back to the farm   most just accept the bush camp realities

guys were sleeping in the kitchen until those other bunks showed up, middle

of the night, cold as hell, we made a fire and were surprised no rcmp

hid the dope under two hundred pound bolt kegs   rolled them in

mock races to keep warm threw a million rocks   tried not to look scared

in the distance a farmer's light-years away

white hats usually everywhere all anxious to make a name for themselves

and go to work no matter what, before the crazy cooks fall off of the pas-

senger too

don't be stupid, kid   they will give U free coveralls, gloves and good

work boots if U can prove U got a job, ask the welfare guy   nobody

will hire U in runners, kid, you are in steel toe country now

hide your feet or something   else they will send U home   there is

an old pair kicking around the I O office   scoop those boots, kid

whatever

Johnny watches this extra-young guy all excited by this city gig,

trying too hard to be cool, trying like hell to pile lumber

clumsy but strong he shows him better and the kid actually listens

Johnny thinks back to when he was the kid and

after working steady Johnny pulls out a quiet smoke   and gives

'em one but real quietly, he was not bumming smokes   five at a

time   the other guys desperado wallets yawning

besides if U are too generous, then U are not street

Johnny was street bush sorter in-between

Lotsa bush camp

Laborer of Fortune   Fortune's Heel

last to volunteer   but   first to the spike hammer   strong

physical   always hunter aware   hunted stare.

If U work I O on Friday U get paid on Friday   a nearby bar

always cashes the checks   why not   many go straight into

the beer barn   cool zone blinkers on and looking at the ground

safer in the dimly lit environs   nowhere else to go

no ID required   just put your X here

just like a treaty thinks Johnny

spiker or nipper

now on the railroad, basically you are one of two things

A. a spiker

B. a nipper

Everybody has seen the long nosed spike hammer, elegant func-

tional for sure, driving in that last golden spike, the spikers had

favorite hammers that they kept all season, those who were getting

bushed gave their hammer a name, some like those new long-

handled fibreglass ones that give whip to the blow, newfangled but
better than hard wood

The slow, inferior nipper just keeps the tie and tie plate snug while
the stately spiker concentrates on a one inch square with all energy,
looks spectacular when U hit the spike, and god awful stupid and
loud when U miss, especially when U break the hammer

after all
John Henry was a steel driving man
nippers are never elite, usually heavy set, bewhiskered and befud-
dled and bewildered at best.
Spikers can be divas   they made room for you on the motor car
at the end of the day
a crossing spike, long and mean lean, separates the pretenders from
the contenders.
Johnny was a spiker
liked the finality   either you hit the spike or you missed
everything prepared for him
and it was real railroad somehow   a masculine rhythm to spiking
everyone had to keep their distance when that HAMMER
COMES DOWN, that made the day go past quicker, the satisfying
sound of three hits per spike.
when you become a spiker you become a railroad lifer even when
they did lay all of you off.

welfare shuffle

Johnny sees a certain walk downtown

a take your own goddamn time 'tude

where U don't walk in straight lines

close to an aimless   shuffle

carrying a heavy load with empty pockets alone and nobody cares

creates this down the tubes shuffle

of waiting in a soup line and everyone driving by knows that and

stare without comprehension

without tolerance

the dry food of the breadline   economic drought

the borderline between stale and the other

looking away quick in case U are contagious

eats away at 'struggling novelist' psyche

Johnny always worked   physical hard   wood and water

thinks of his uncle

INTERLUDE II

(only a poet can interlude anytime   it is an honor to be called poet
Johnny uncleDreams   Jenny dreams the same dream, same time,
different perspective did not matter   even in the food bank line
J and J keep cool   together that first instant happy   Johnny
writes and talks and laughs and always scrapes enough for coffee
somehow   dead end job wizard financial   eat what is front of
you and shutup   Jenny looks for work in newspapers   while
Johnny writes about his northern uncle)

hydro babies
all washed out
those hydro babies never
cry
they just gurgle
they can swim
like fuck

trees lurk underwater
smiling wet dreams

I just hate this
wet look

Bush Voices

Jenny gets used to those soft g syllables   off side voices self
instruct   learn by watching
she watches a tree grow
floating log verbiage   colors   torpedo-shifting nuance as
river muscles by

the gang wonders why she dares to go off the track
I wouldn't get away with that was the general mutter
besides, what about the
wood freaking ticks !!!!!!!!!!!!!!
the dreaded Puncture Bug invisible except to the city mind

private male thoughts: what if U got lost?!

Jenny watches out for the city ticks instead

she visits the cruise missile   brings it flowers   keeps it company
she wants to name it
she hopes that it belongs to her, somehow
why is she the one
doing the spike lee   right thing
when will she see Johnny again
muskeg power creeps to the edge of the tracks
entice
she follows the flats by the river and starts to see things especially
animal tracks
bush signposts scream information
to a country dog's nose

to someone who sees the story in natural tones, to the poet that
lurks in us
she can feel the snares of civilization

INTERLUDE III

mouse trap number nine

come one
come all
welcome
welcome to this house of mine
have no fear
take a chance
let me invite you
delight you
positively excite you
enter don't ever forget
that you met
mouse trap number nine

----

or very likely a northern pose:

yep   for sure, for sure   for sure it is plain as day

it's a female moose calf track all right
can't you see?
looks left-pawed   tired or hurt
see how this hoof drags?
U learn to read   tracks by looking at tracks in the bush
U read erdrich tracks and wonder more

can't U see that?   Look at the tracks
tracks are left behind   loaded historical markers

Northerners know this
the work up north migration always creates the
Innate Ability of Males Who Suddenly Become   Indian-Like
in the sacred, macho, dead freaking serious
How to Read Tracks/How to Read and Personally Handle Animal
Feces/and Tell (shoot a cranberry off your head) the track History
and Story about the Animal   known as the infamous Huntin'/
Fishin'/Trappin'/Bush
Pro Syndrome
found in your jeans
be aware of north of 60 BS in a south of the beaver belt society

but the guys did the usual creosote workin' route. They had no
choice.

Jenny follows her own tracks to the missile.

sadly, in a small tight grouping, the hierarchal white hats watch
Jenny walk off into the bush while the muttering, yellow hats
suspiciously peer from
behind a boxcar
easier when she was gone they agreed heatedly, while each one
secretly stares at her body
guys started performing when she neared
got mad easier took no teasing when she was around
did not want to be seen taking orders
were not working then.
better, that she goes to the bush thinks the lead white hat, as the
lesser white hats hastily agree
lighting a smoke, sucking caffeine, looking for keys, getting ready
for iron-clad, tin-minded, holy, work rituals to take over. It is so, so,
ever so long until layoff time, think the white hats sadly.

Jenny knows that something is a-hoof
this missile is the centre   a large gatheringof tracks every night
all animal   all over the place
the tracks lead her where those bush voices echo
Johnny sends her a letter with loving hand drawn illustrations of
assorted animal tracks and Jenny sleeps with these under her pillow.
Jenny now is learning how to read

dream alphabet crosses syllabic sounds

cahkasinaham

ᒫᑂᑿᕐᐊᑂᐊᒼ

(s/he/it writes in cree syllabics)

these symbols surround her bunk
she hits the bush

petroglyph rock art one oh one
winter count apprentice
Inukshuk designer fonts
dictionary floats oral

a track is the storyteller

animal tracks, sidewalk cracks, word attacks, goodbye union jacks

Johnny wanted to make sure that the tracks that he sent to Jenny
were faithful to his memories

He scores a box of sidewalk chalk and begins to draw assorted
animal tracks on that huge slab of cement outside city hall
This does not go down with the security
they hose down the drawings in front of a jeering crowd, mostly
young, and

Then this flash-frozen-from-the-sixties usual guy, who
automatically has this second hand books/styrocoffee/old
cassettes, older overflowing ashtrays/poetry and acoustic music
joint

This guy likes Johnny's "urban Cree approach" lets him draw in
front of his store and gives him a tip jar and Johnny also quick

draw mcgraws pieces of
animal like the crow quill
or other important feathers
the skeletal aspect of animals
like he used to in the boredom of his uncle's snowbound
trapper's cabin

and
he leaves that industrial overload gig for now

People, flashing cash, want their portrait done
Make me look tough, okay man?
I want you to capture my true spirit

Johnny allies them with certain animals
as he got better and better with the chalk
It was easy
If he didn't like them he put their face on a skunk
or as a dog licking his ass
Johnny almost got his own ass kicked for that one.

It was easy to read the crowd
Guys wanted to be wolves, eagles, maybe a wolverine
Women wanted birds
Kids love them all
Even worms

He drew sidewinder snake tracks   huge and neon
leading right up to the local cash your check/ mail box/ address
for the homeless/ for drifters/ rip-off store

This made it to the papers
but he never got famous from sidewalking art
just got stepped on once in awhile

Johnny began to create union jax in unflattering ways
Like on a roll of toilet paper
Or emitting from a hypo
because he had to salute that flag every morning
when he was a kid in a leather strapped school for speaking his
language

Most passer-bys hardly recognized this flag
When asked what he was doing Johnny gave obscure answers:
Cuz of that muskeg tea and spruce gum and all that
They threw money and left him alone

His hand guided by bush memories   chopping wood
socks for gloves
Of the joy of gasoline birch bark flame
Of spruce sticky smell and how
easy wood split sounds at thirty below

his husky chasing spruce partridge for school lunches and how
they laughed at him
of five long rifle 22 shells and you better come back with some-
thing to eat
a single shot cooey had a special place on the wall
snaring rabbits and trading them for smokes
he drew all this while the city closes in from all sides

His drawing utensils howl

Prairie Steppenwolf

Was ist daß ?

Prairie Steppenwolf?

What is that?

A new kind of howl

Different than Ginsberg

Still a mad generation

Slinks through chicken house of life

Yapping sounds

The coyote   the coyote

Survivor urban rural dog

Keeps tricking   us

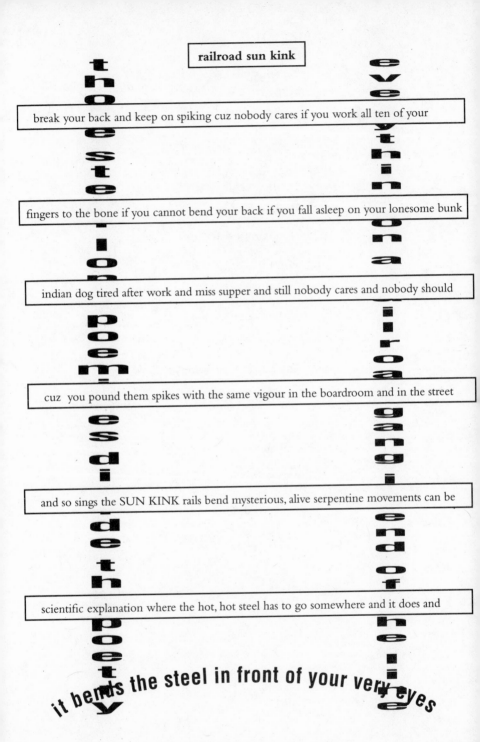

railroad sun kink

break your back and keep on spiking cuz nobody cares if you work all ten of your

fingers to the bone if you cannot bend your back if you fall asleep on your lonesome bunk

indian dog tired after work and miss supper and still nobody cares and nobody should

cuz you pound them spikes with the same vigour in the boardroom and in the street

and so sings the SUN KINK rails bend mysterious, alive serpentine movements can be

scientific explanation where the hot, hot steel has to go somewhere and it does and

it bends the steel in front of your very eyes

56

downtown trapline

giving up on escalators Johnny got busy learning the city ways

What sign are U?
Johnny looked her up and down: 'bear sign' he sez cool-like, and walked away smooth and sure, leaving his bush signs.

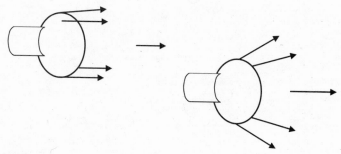

What kind of car do U drive?
{Proud}
A Pontiac Strato Chief. Uhmm, and an Aztec, or a Chinook/ Apache chopper, or mebbe, sometimes I ride a Bronco or a Mustang or I dodge a Pony, fit an Arrow, or even a Cherokee. Or I dodge a Dakota, or ride the Cheyenne, but the best ride, is the cnn bareback tomahawk missile

What's your occupation?
Well, first a couple of hints then a fill-in-the-blank to help you along.
Hint 1: I don't like cowboys, as a rule anyway.
Hint 2: I ride horses, always bareback and usually a paint/pinto/ occasionally appaloosa.
Fill in the BLANK: doctor, lawyer, _____ _____ .
Three guesses, and that is it.

First two don't remount.

        Johnny asleep, alone   that nite.

feeling that blue

you know you are feeling blue
when
your pubic hair is older than your boss
when you used to
baby-sit his older sister
and she is pregnant
and the ultrasound proves that the kid
looks like your landlord

and he needs your room now
you know you are feeling blue
when you have to change provinces
so you can get utilities
when your luggage is mostly card bored

when you start looking at that
greyhound driver like he was your dear old dad
you just have to be feeling blue
when your relatives give you gift certificates
from out of town

and your ass is really really blue
when going to a food court is a big night on the town
when alley graffiti is like your
aerosol version of the bible

when all park benches are booked with your
friends
and you wear white running shoes all
winter long
and you think the left bank
is your bank account

when money mart is kind of cool place
to do your income tax cuz
it is warm there
your ass is freaking blue when you shop for groceries at seven eleven
cuz they follow everybody around
not just you
oh thank heaven

you got those blues
when a career in the sally ann seems to be a logical choice
so blue you blow a breathalyser to see how many beers you had
forgotten
the night before
and your oldest, best buddy
paints swastikas on your girl friend's
ass
and she likes it and you like it too cuz now at least you get some
weird attention

now that's the freaking blues
too blue to be a loser
when you live the blues
without the music

Johnny wanders alone feeling the street vibes
jesus look-alikes ask for money
nanabush plastic shaman shams wrestle for big bucks and for the hearts of
little bucks

Soup for the Hood

Time for a food bank poem

Brother   Can you spare me a potato?

Slice those carrots thin

Feed me   feed me   feed me

Join bellies first

Before minds canned meat

Mr. Grocery man

Sets on potato hill

Yukon Gold looking down

Pile gets fat

Shrinks within

Core so rotten

So do not try to hide the hungry   Because potatoes got

eyes.

He wanders erratic happy in turbulent
He thinks of Jenny
Writes poetry on sidewalk chalk temporal

real furby[1]

since we split up I live on furby street

not easy sleeping with fire extinguisher
those collectible cute furbies
nowhere fuzzy not here not once
easy bake neighborhood fries furniture

forever dog daze

real furby   this spring   this summer   this winter   this spring

heats up the whole damn

town

meanwhile back on the gang

stretch was stretching, serious chawing on a piece of wood,

reaching for a day off, has rubs up alongside the steel rail and

concrete tie universe, used to being alone, stretch likes the gang,

his chawing philosophy clandestine arena of thought, the way he

likes it, his seeming torpor hides the arresting thinking, new boots

or new coveralls on payday becomes important when this is your

only job, when weather bites and scratches undeniable, stretch

once pondered untried ways to become a popular mechanic, yet,

being one of the boys don't count when there are no women

thinks stretch

---

1 Note: for those out of town: out of touch: furby street is the 'hood'

newfie met some outport screech (as night as owl) and the bush,
about freaking time he thinks, and felt at home, relived some of
the local island dance fights, had pogey daydreams sitting, waiting
for the mail-godot, EI night dreams, questions he cannot answer,
like how are any of your relatives: he knows they are survivor pro
extraordinaire, instead he prays in his rum way to be laid off, had
outport roots that gurgle and spin across seasonal spans, always from
out of town, never works at home, the new found migration rock
expulsion, rite of male passage: work up north, out west, and try
not to drink yourself to death, all this new found cash needed back
home too

frenchie was long gone by now   he was drifting alone
now wishes he still was eating on the gang
thumb out in the yellowhead hiway
looking   lookout for the horsehead nebula
when cars zip by   stellar gas of orion mixes with leaded
the horseshoe nebula   galloping star trax supreme walking on
dotted lines
Ω Ω

          Ω Ω

                    Ω Ω

frenchie alone that night

heading east, not hitching both sides of the road, outta alberta again

red, always resourceful, read a book of instructional fly fishing,

found a dictionary of trout flies and bored everyone with mundane

details: what hair works best with muddy bottoms, his favorite trout

fly, those hackle details, rummage of fishy materials, the complexi-

ties of hook sizes, and hook parts: like the bend, the throat, the

gape, the barb, the shank, the eye, and the all-important point, just

imagine the fish mouth, hook come alive, craftsman terms, human

words inscribe killing machine, zen and the art of fish homicide,

hidden away in delicate feather of fly tying, or, in certain, covert-

to-the-max circles, insect bondage, red the specialist, demands,

needs, others, to his passion, never actually been fly fishing, bought

spanking new hip boots on payday, wishes for a fly tying vise, made

plans for the specialist scissors: deer scissors for deer hair, midge

scissors for the most discrete inconspicuous flies, curved scissors for

shaping

just so fish stories   hackle pliers   bobbin holders

practice casting alongside the track, snags ties, hard hats

happily royal coachman attitude suddenly emerges, his LL. sardine

(weird cousin to L.L. bean hat) now submerged in homemade flies,

a dangerously sharp hat,

red was growing

sparks came back with a southern disease but soon got over it, he

hooks up an ingenious method of grabbing radio waves and here

way back in the canadian shield that was worth something but

he only liked homey dokey radio talk shows but still he strung

a speaker onto the roof of his bunk and became cool, as others

gather to grasp an audio glimpse of home, maybe, as they gather

smoking, BS-ing and jawing the nite away, as lonely respect is paid

to these distant voices and sounds, 70s late nite music filters the

bush

the head white hat began to manufacture a skinning knife from a

used rail saw blade, one that lost its teeth, old now in this industrial

disease

the all-important tang needs this good steel, tempered male

and creates beer bottle openers from spikes, great at parties (those

grizzled days before the twist caps: 'the church key')

somehow still proud of this gang and

soon others followed suit, something to do besides getting hosed

after all this white hat was from the same small town

the scchhht scchhht of knife sharpening, arkansas stone steady, adds

to the night-time sounds

a finality noise

it was macho enough to get artistic

unexpectedly the railroad skinning knife olympix begins, new blades, not the dull useless ones, began to disappear from the tool

car one by one

then emerge suddenly in this unspoken competition

meanwhile

the bull cook got into chatelaine magazine quietly and deeply and

all consuming undiscovered area of his life

clipping choice recipes for that laid off winter

he saw the remains of his life spent on newly discovered crafts

suddenly he got aim

and, as for the perfessor, who really was a lost, lost grad student,

he stopped reading and got very oral, and burns his books one by

freaking one and nobody notices, after all, bushed was bushed, and

this guy couldn't hit the damn spike anyway

and on the gang that was what really counted

the cook, the third one this year

typical gang cook he got mad when he had to cook something

he had this beaded leather sling and he walks along the track when

he had time off expels crushed official rock into the timeless   bush

a blue collar david slaying goliath of boredom   rock crash startle

awakens that which never sleeps   the voiceless bush

undeclares sound missiles to those who listen

turns out that this cook was wanted

not by his ex either

no cook, he left in a typical quit-the-gang-tradition-mode

no goodbyes, no nothing, long walk to town, maybe tears into

soundless word angers

I freaking quit, cook your own goddam eggs, that will teach you to mess

with my bunk, my mind, my fears, my lowly non-existent hard hat

no breakfast cuz the cookies all hid out, seen it before

no work today

but the cook was led into a cruiser owing money on bar tabs

somewhere

so

an unexpected day off   gift from the railroad gods

everyone shower scrambles

some polish boots full of hope

comb hair   go to town before it was too late

and as for jenny

she finds a medicine bag hanging mute on her door

she grasps it   feels the beads

somehow knew not to look inside

she senses many tracks outside her bunk

bush tracks

she makes trax

the bull cook falls in love

jenny's bunk has been made 'just so' lately

her floor   window sparkle wash

extra (brand new) blankets metamorphose despite the trailer heat

surprising new electric kettle with all the caffeine fixings

an empty coffee can bursting flowers and glint metallic was the last

clue

head over steel toes thinks jenny

the bull cook sits too close to her at meals

passes her every freaking thing twice

could be handy   *could really suck*

when the bull cook falls in love

one of the chatelaines

how-to crafts language

placebo homemade gifts

instead of love

railroad love is a spike pounded with steel   undulating

waver of lines in the distance

kinda like there is love way over there   by those dogs there

the bull cook took up embroidery

rough and dauphin but embroidery none-the-less

bandanna   embroidery born somewhere on the railroad trax

a fistful of spikes and beside-the-track flowers

clandestinely picked

fit the blue ribbon vase

the bull cook bought a proud new work shirt

snappy silver snap buttons   cowpoke[2] without the horse

rolled up at the sleeve as he cleaned toilets

mail order square dance shoes at the polish

brushed up on his polka skills

boiled his long lost comb in a tin pail

quickly followed by camp fire preen into a jagged piece of mirror

the water appears atwood poisonous

later he switched magazines   worried that he may get caught

(most are surprised that he can read)

finds the common fishin'/huntin' info he needs

catches a ride to the local macleod store (three miles

on gravel road first

---

2 Maybe in the bush dictionary 'cowpoke' is someone who:
   1. pokes cows. Not there! You know, just safe masculine pokes, cattle prods, push that bush.
   2. polkas cows? An outdoor 'fall in the campfire' kind of a night; often thinly disguised as a knight in loser armour made of brown glass, falls off of his freaking horse in front of the freaking king.
   3. stopped serious poking in the mid 70s, ran out of cows, now, a preferential horseflesh.
   4. polka dot bandannas are not even close. Don't fence me out!

then the hitchhike to town. Love .... sigh)

gets a tree stand, you know, the kind that real hunters use, a detach-

able seat that hang-sits in a tree, and you await, camouflage-assed,

perfect, you wait, none of this slogging it up and down hills in

dense bush, the deer may have ears, but the treed hunter has eagle

advantage

the bull cook sneaks out

puts his treestand close to where jenny works

sits quiet yet tremendously excited

embroidering

protective

notes who pays too much attention to jenny

no clean bunk for them or for a second offence, no hot water

weird goings up there

the bull cook sits up there battles squirrels in his new comfort zone

this is railroad love

this is not what jenny imagines when johnny told her

to watch her back

trax

johnny abandons art for jenny

he sees that he is artless

that art don't count for much when you sit in rooming house/

the strip hotel   watch others watch you do nothing but suck-

ing thumbs and rolling yet one more smoke, one more look at the

empty downtown streets at nite

then art is not in your being

art is not luxury

it is ugly art, all the warts, all the insides

lips and hips

this guy from muskeg country usually doesn't have a chance when his

seclusion   his perspective   only works walking in muskeg soft   few allow that same cachet   as that wall street three step

first shaky stttttttep

those lips must be heard with the mind and especially with the

second step

it is so   piHHip   to be a heart   shape when
your lake carries that name   and meet those hips   on love street
on that plateau of moving image they may intersect

may sink together
and away and alongside   another   that is the way of the **muskeg**

l i p s a n d m u s k e g a n d h i p s

Treestand

it
aint
easy sitting
in a
gummy spruce tree
alone 'cept your trusty antler obsessed
deer gun scope electronic woodcraft (shoot
from another freaking county from
way over there these days)
hunter is not the
word for selling bear bladder for what? for who? and why the hell
for?
you have to make a stand
you have to choose between the
ways in
the woods
the forest
to
keep
on
tree
standing

I was a teen-age gandy dancer

some of those switch ties were sixteen feet long

drag them half sand buried up the grade   slippery like guts

two guys per tie   very democratic   my partner didn't seem to understand anything

so I had to be the brains of this outfit

black bundles of ties metal strap flash

industrial creosote-wood hinge, railroad inukshuk

pick up a tie

any tie will do

put it in the right place

while the envied 'tie straighteners' always made some small
adjustment

then you pick up another tie

put it in the right place

your partner continues inane monologue about him and his
drinkin' buddies

pick up a tie . . . put it in the right place . . . pick up a tie . . .

crow court

jenny tracks through the bush, avoiding the willow whips, not too

many bugs, the trax appear luminous, while a select trio of crows

air amble above her, tracking her cacophonous arrogant

meanwhile slip-sliding, hurrying along, worried and frantic, the

bull cook follows her from a distance, gear clinking

the crows, amazed at his conspicuous, know that he is not of the bush but harmless

it is time for crow court

jenny emanates key witness

the three judges

(after all crows group in murders so there is strong need for court)

line up on favorite twig overlooking that silver intruder, that cruise

missile acknowledge their fans, ten pace the cruise intruder,

while fur, fin, feather,

gather solemn

and begin their judgement

1. James Crow : ultraconservative

2. Sally Crow : up-and-comer in the rank

3. āhāsis ▷ "ᐧ▷ᕀ∆∩ (baby crow)

Jenny, somehow fluent in crow, somehow glib in bush culture,

serene upon the carefully selected stump that was her witness chair,

gets to see the track makers from makswa (bear) to old,

cranky turtles

she sits think-ponders of Johnny and his city mapping

children of the cement

my childhood background stretches

landscape wild beyond sight beyond the NWT beyond me

come see our beer bottle forest, it grows bigger

brown X-mas trees for sale or refund or to break

soft rabbit sounds, loud tracks reverb

can it be a. . . wolverine, a lost trapper?

tracks on the arms, in the neck in the eye

long lost dad jumping like a bunny

water games, do you know the hair/thread snake of northern water?

fish rainbow gleam, homemade fishing rod, cattail weaves, self

fire hydrant delight, rainbow peons, stray cat running

fish for spare change, food bank animal

baby ducks familiar, run free as long as you can, as you want to

tree ripples wind ripples love ripples

baby duck, gimli goose, apple jack, ripple wine,

runs over souls, mallard breakdown

see the men pour over the child

see the cement harden

hypodermic sand toys

see the   *children of the cement*

johnny keeps his trap antennae aquiver

mouse trap number nine

Thank u Page

Dedicate

Cily

Bush Camp Stories

Ab Writ. Collective
Urb, Shaman
M Writers Guild

Snooks

John Francis
Brian Vick
Mike Hartung
Cliff thot
M. Morris ?
J. Robert F.

David Streit

UAM & UAW
profs. & students

my family
- Georgie
- Rob
- Doro
- John
  Peter

art Galleries = V Pool
etc. → m Print Assoc.
& those individuals
from there

! Other poets &
gang workers
- a way 1 life
gone now

Urb
Cool
Poet

Literary
- CV 2 = Contemporary Verse 2
- Conundrums (newsletter U Shaman)
- Zygote
- P. Fire

Marvin Francis
1955–2005